What This Book Will Do for You

This book will show you how to use constructive confrontation, effective communication techniques, and action planning to manage most conflicts or potential conflicts. It will also help you keep ordinary disagreements and differences of opinion or values from erupting into conflict.

Other Titles in the Successful Office Skills Series

Becoming an Effective Leader
Building Better Relationships on the Job
Coaching and Counseling in the Workplace
Creative Problem Solving
Effective Team Building
Get Organized! How to Control Your Life Through Self-Management
How to Be a Successful Interviewer
How to Be a Successful Manager
How to Deal With Difficult People
How to Delegate Effectively
How to Get the Best Out of People
How to Make an Effective Speech or Presentation
How to Negotiate a Raise or Promotion
How to Read Financial Statements
How to Run a Meeting
How to Write Easily and Effectively
How to Write an Effective Résumé
Improve Your Reading Power
Increasing Your Memory Power
Making Tough Decisions
Managing Stress
Polishing Your Professional Image
Winning on the Telephone

CONFLICT RESOLUTION

Donald H. Weiss

amacom
American Management Association

New York • Atlanta • Boston • Chicago • Kansas City • San Francisco • Washington, D.C.
Brussels • Toronto • Mexico City

> This book is available at a special
> discount when ordered in bulk quantities.
> For information, contact Special Sales Department,
> AMACOM, a division of American Management Association,
> 135 West 50th Street, New York, NY 10020.

This publication is designed to provide accurate and authoritative information in regard to the subject matter covered. It is sold with the understanding that the publisher is not engaged in rendering legal, accounting, or other professional service. If legal advice or other expert assistance is required, the services of a competent professional person should be sought.

Library of Congress Cataloging-in-Publication Data

Weiss, Donald H., 1936–
    Conflict resolution / Donald H. Weiss.
      p. cm. — (The successful office skills series)
    Includes bibliographical references and index.
    ISBN 0-8144-7820-4
    1. Conflict management. I. Title. II. Series.
HD42.W44 1993
650.1'3—dc20   93-10603
                                                  CIP

© 1993 AMACOM, a division of
American Management Association, New York.
All rights reserved.
Printed in the United States of America.

This publication may not be reproduced,
stored in a retrieval system,
or transmitted in whole or in part,
in any form or by any means, electronic,
mechanical, photocopying, recording, or otherwise,
without the prior written permission of AMACOM,
a division of American Management Association,
135 West 50th Street, New York, NY 10020.

Printing number

10 9 8 7 6 5 4 3 2 1

CONTENTS

Introduction — 1

CHAPTER ONE
Disagreements and Conflicts — 2

CHAPTER TWO
Constructive Confrontation — 8

CHAPTER THREE
Effective Communication — 13

CHAPTER FOUR
Giving Feedback — 22

CHAPTER FIVE
Listening to Feedback — 28

CHAPTER SIX
Mediating Between Warring Factions — 35

CHAPTER SEVEN
Taking Action — 44

Conclusion	52
Suggested Readings	53
Index	55
About the Author	58

INTRODUCTION

It would be wonderful if we never had to deal with conflicts. If people could work out their disagreements in peace and with goodwill, they could disagree with each other, share differences of opinions and values, share scarce rewards with one another, and never fight over anything. It would be wonderful, but the chances of this happening anytime soon range from slim to none. If you have any doubts, just recall that the death of communist rule in Eastern Europe didn't usher in a golden age in the "liberated" lands, the end to apartheid didn't bring brotherhood and love to South Africa, and peace initiatives in the Middle East haven't put an end to internecine fighting.

We all have to deal with our own struggles, sometimes over nothing more earthshaking than how much space an employee should have in an office or how tall a manager's cubicle walls should be. That's because conflicts on the job often concern disagreements about when, where, and how work should be done and who should do it. Such conflicts become quite serious when they involve what should be done and who should benefit from the work; these conflicts usually come down to a conflict of values. When beliefs or ideas come into conflict, they're relatively easy to resolve because they involve mostly experience-based facts. Conflicts of values, on the other hand, are much more difficult to manage.

Regardless of the nature of the conflict, all conflicts involve differences of opinions, values, goals, or desires. Still, not all such disagreements produce, or need to produce, conflict. Whether ordinary differences produce conflict depends in large part on whether differences are managed creatively and in a way that is healthy for everyone.

This little book will show you how to use constructive confrontation, effective communication techniques, and action planning to help you manage most conflicts or potential conflicts in two different kinds of situations:

1. Conflicts between yourself and other people
2. Conflicts between people with whom you work or whom you supervise

It will also help you keep ordinary disagreements and differences of opinion or values from erupting into conflict.

CHAPTER ONE

Disagreements and Conflicts

∽

Disagreement and conflict are not the same thing. Although all conflicts involve disagreements, not all disagreements erupt into conflict.

Disagreements

For the most part, disagreements are healthy. When they are open and managed in the spirit of friendliness and cooperation, they help people settle their differences and promote creativity or innovation. If necessity is the mother of invention, then disagreement is its father.

When you disagree with someone, what is really behind the dispute? In most cases, your differences involve how each of you sees something; that is, you disagree about the facts in a situation. An old sitcom disagreement between a husband and wife might go something like this:

She: You really don't ever notice anything I wear. I bet you can't even remember what I was wearing the night you proposed.
He: You're on. You were wearing a green dress.
She: Ha! I win. I was wearing a blue dress.
He: You were not. It was green.
She: Was not.
He: Was too.

And that supposedly witty bit of dialogue can go on until the next commercial break.

A more serious disagreement occurs when you and the other person disagree about values. When you disagree about what is good or bad, right or wrong, beautiful or ugly, you tap deep emotions or feelings. When you disagree about these issues, you're talking about ideas you hold dear. Many years ago, the slogan "What's good for General Motors is good for America" pitted even relatives against one another, and the tragedies of the American Civil War in the nineteenth century and the Vietnam War in the twentieth demonstrate how serious a disagreement of values can become.

In short, disagreements occur when people experience the same situation differently or hold different beliefs or values. They see things differently and believe different versions of the same so-called facts. This kind of disagreement often comes up at trials when two eyewitnesses tell different versions of what occurred. Often, even when you and another person agree on the facts, you each interpret them differently or feel differently about them.

All the same, what distinguishes disagreements from conflicts is how these differences are managed, rather than their content. When you discuss your differences with the intent of resolving them in a mutually satisfying manner, you are disagreeing. Discussing differences in this way is a step toward preventing conflict, rather than a symptom of conflict.

Conflicts

Conflict, unlike disagreement, is not healthy. It usually erupts because disagreements haven't been open, friendly, or cooperative. Conflicts involve disagreements about what is true, good, or beautiful but differ from simple disagreements in that at least one person believes, rightly or wrongly, that his right to satisfy his needs or his interest have been denied. What might have started out as a simple disagreement turns into "fightin' words."

From Disagreement to Conflict

I'm going to illustrate how people get into conflicts and then manage them by dramatizing an actual situation that wasn't healthy for anyone.

Alice and May are two claim adjusters for a property and casualty insurance company. Alice has always been, let's say, difficult to handle. She's been having some personal problems lately that have not affected her work—until this morning. Still, the battle begins with what seems to be a minor incident.

Alice: May?
May: Yes. Are you okay, Alice?
Alice: Well, yes, but I'm not able to come in today. Would you tell Barbara for me?
May: What should I tell her?
Alice: Make up something creative, would you? I can't even think straight today.
May: What's wrong?
Alice: Nothing, really. It's just one of those days for me.

It has been "just one of those days" for Alice for quite a while. This is the third time this month she hasn't been "able to come in today." But on those other occasions, she has told Barbara, their boss, herself. Everyone thinks that Alice may have a drinking problem, but, if she does, she has never shown it in the office. However, she has been absent quite a bit over the last six months, and she's often late when she does come in.

Alice: And handle the Dobbs and the Bitten files for me, will you? That's a dear. I'll talk with you later. Thanks, May. You're a great friend. [*Before May can respond, Alice hangs up.*]

In her frustration, May throws the phone back into its cradle.

May: What a nerve. First she wants me to lie for her, then she wants me to close two tough claims files.

One of the cases, Dobbs, may involve fraud. May scans the files stacked on her own desk. She can barely see past them to the surface below. No way.

The claim adjuster reaches for her phone.

May [*thinking*]: I'll call her back and tell her no on both counts, but. . . . [*She has second thoughts.*] If Alice does come in today, she'll be hell on earth. If I don't help her out, she'll never do anything to help me. Yet I can't lie to Barbara, and there's no way to handle those two files today.

May doesn't lie to Barbara. She just doesn't tell the whole story.

May: She just called in and told me she couldn't make it in. No, I don't know what's wrong. The Dobbs and Bitten files? I know they have to be closed today. I guess I'll handle them.

May does it all. She stays late to finish her own work, but she closes Alice's files on time by turning the Dobbs file over to an external investigator and notifying him of her action. She then settles with Bitten for half of what he thinks his claim is worth.

Well, our claim adjuster is a pro at handling potential conflicts over claims, but when it comes to interpersonal relations, she's not quite as adept. Then again, not too many people can handle an Alice very easily.

When a Disagreement Becomes a Conflict

May and Alice might agree on the bare-bones facts—that Alice called May to ask May to cover for her. But they are joined in conflict no matter how much they agree on the basic facts and on the rightness or wrongness of how Alice treated May.

May experiences what has happened as conflict because she believes that Alice has trampled on her rights—her right to remain outside the supervisor-employee relationship between Barbara and Alice, her right to be honest, her right to get her own work done, her right to do only the work assigned to her. Alice may never know how May feels, but the conflict exists. The question is, what does May do about this situation?

She could do nothing, but obviously that will leave the conflict unresolved. How does she resolve the conflict? First, she has to involve Alice in a discussion of the situation: constructive confrontation. Second, she has to ensure that they communicate with each other in a way that allows both of them to understand and to deal with the issues between them. Third, she'll have to work at a resolution, rather than just let the conversation end everything. Left on their own, conflicts don't just go away—they get worse.

CHAPTER TWO

Constructive Confrontation

Many people have been taught to hide differences of opinion, feelings, or values. Remember when Thumper, the little rabbit in the Disney movie version of *Bambi*, laughed at other critters and poked fun? Remember his mother's admonition? "If you don't have nothin' nice to say, don't say nothin' at all." Well, Thumper's mom may have given him some bad advice.

Suppressed differences don't go away. They surface when you least expect them or least want them to show up—usually when you're in the middle of a major project with tight deadlines. The stress does it. The stress strips away the façade you build to cover your feelings, and little things became major catastrophes. Contrary to what Mama Rabbit suggests, it's better to deal with differences when they occur than to say nothing at all.

There are four ways of dealing with conflict: constructive confrontation, confrontation for the sake of domination, avoidance, and compromise. Older but still useful labels for these four strategies are I win–you win, I win–you lose, I lose–you win, and I lose–you lose. Of the four, only the I win–you win strategy, or constructive confrontation, helps to resolve conflict.

Confrontation for the Sake of Domination

Alice breezes in the next day, meets briefly with Barbara, and storms up to May's desk.

Alice: Why didn't you tell Barbara something more creative than "I don't know what's wrong"? She was all over me.
May: I couldn't just lie.
Alice: Next time, think about what you're doing to me.

With that, Alice flounces over to her desk and drops heavily into her chair. End of conversation. She has said her piece, made her demands, and, as far as she is concerned, nothing more need be said. That's the I win–you lose strategy.

This strategy is characterized by aggressiveness. Frequently, the confrontation is angry and bitter. No problems are actually addressed, and the conflict is suppressed, rather than resolved.

Sometimes the attempt to dominate is an exercise in power. Some supervisors feel that the only way to succeed is to use confrontation for the sake of dominating the employees reporting to them. They're demanding, argumentative, stubborn, and unfriendly.

What such supervisors seem to forget is that the position of supervisor, by itself, bestows power on them. It's called *status* power; that is, by virtue of their positions, they can control subordinates' lives, as well as the compensation and the rewards the subordinates get for what they do. Supervisors have the status to demand what they want. Most supervisors have learned that using (read misusing) their power to dominate is a mistake. They force their employees to take the same stance May took at first: avoiding confrontation whenever possible.

Avoidance

May is stunned. She has received no thank you for what she did, only Alice's anger at her for not having lied. May sits there at her desk, feeling frustrated and flustered, not doing anything, not saying anything. In fact, she resolves not to talk to Alice again—unless she has to.

This is a classic case of avoidance, a you win–I lose strategy. I win–you lose and you win–I lose are companion strategies; one won't work without the other. This situation is quite different from "distancing," which is a successful technique for dealing with high emotions or complex problems.

When you distance yourself from someone, you let things cool down a little. You step back, take a deep breath, and take a good hard look at the problem before returning to the fray. But Alice isn't doing that. Instead, by vowing not to talk to Alice unless she has to, she's refusing (at this point) to deal with the conflict. Ultimately, everyone will lose: I lose–you lose.

Compromise

Avoidance may *lead* to a lose–lose result, but compromise is an I lose–you lose strategy right from the start. "If she'd make up the lie and tell me what to say," May thinks to herself, "I'd be telling Barbara only what I know. That's not the same as lying, is it? But, then, Alice would have to get with the program or I won't do it."

If May follows through on this approach, she'll be compromising her principles and demanding that Alice make changes in her behavior that she may not be able to make at this time. That's what compromise is all about.

It's a you lose–I lose strategy in which everyone gives up something or concedes a need, rather than working together to meet everyone's needs. Everyone loses something in the process. In addition, like avoidance, compromise suppresses conflict, rather than dealing with it. No one gets anything out of that.

Constructive Confrontation

The only strategy that gets all the issues out on the table completely and enables you to deal with them completely is *constructive confrontation*, which is defined as confrontation for the sake of problem solving. May decides that she will give this strategy a try.

May steps over to Alice's desk and speaks as quietly and as pleasantly as she can.

May: I'm probably as angry with you as you are with me, and I think we need to talk about the situation as soon as we can. I'd like to see a positive solution here, because whatever's preventing you from getting to work is beginning to create a problem for me. I want to help you, but I don't like lying, and I don't like having to close files for you when all I have is secondhand information. Besides, I wound up having to stay until 7:30 last night just to finish up my own work.

Alice [*taken aback by May's candor*]: I'm sorry I shouted at you. I've got some problems at home, that's all. I'll try to make it on time from now on. [*Alice wants to talk with May, but if she does, she'll have to tell her what is going on at home, and that would be difficult.*]

May: I don't think that's enough. Let's meet at lunch. I won't pry, but we have to come to an understanding and decide what to do about this.

Now, this is a good start at an I win–you win strategy. It's designed to bring all issues out on the table in order to resolve them through consensus.

What makes constructive confrontation work is partly a matter of intent. May wants a positive resolution to the conflict, and intentions must be positive. Her strategy is win-win, a necessary condition for confrontation to be constructive. Good faith in all things from all people involved is essential for successful negotiations of differences. However, good intentions without actions mean very little.

She has also acted assertively. She has let her rights drive her decision to talk with Alice, but she has taken Alice's needs or rights into consideration, as well. Assertiveness, rather than aggression, makes discussion possible, and what makes assertiveness different from aggression is, in part, the fact that assertive people recognize the rights of others, as well as their own. In addition, unlike aggression, assertion discloses feelings, rather than masking them in self-righteousness or in other high-handed attitudes.

Unlike the strategy of domination, constructive confrontation calls upon you to use your personal power at all times. Especially if you're a supervisor, you will want to adopt this strategy when resolving conflicts with others. You will want to influence others, rather than forcing them into avoidance or compromise. You will want them to feel good about the results of your disagreement, rather than resenting what happened.

May intends to reach a solution that works for both Alice and herself. She's striving for the necessary ingredient that makes constructive confrontation work: coalescing, a coming together, which is the basis for collaboration. In simplest terms, constructive confrontation does not work without cooperation; both parties must be willing to work on the problem. Good faith and a spirit of cooperation start the process, invest the process with a positive climate for change, and make the process work.

To negotiate successfully, however, both parties have to work at communicating with each other. We'll see just how successful May and Alice are (or aren't) communicating in the chapters to come.

CHAPTER THREE

Effective Communication

෴

Did this ever happen to you? You're having a somewhat general conversation with someone. A few specific comments are made that touch on a raw nerve, on some concern of yours, but that seem pretty plain vanilla—nothing to get excited about. But then the other person says something that brings a flush to your face. You can feel your jaws stiffen. Then you say something, and her voice gets a little louder. Suddenly you're into a full blown argument—and no one knows how it happened. If this has never happened to you, you need to write your own book.

A slip of the tongue, a miscued response, a personal turn of phrase, a personal value—all of these ordinary conversational elements can turn a discussion into a shouting match. Therefore, it seems pretty obvious that any deliberate constructive confrontation can degenerate into conflict unless you deal with differences in perspective and create a climate conducive to resolving conflicts. These two communication skills can help you manage an otherwise difficult situation.

No two people live in the *same* world. Everyone sees and hears the world from different perspectives.

Your reality reflects what's important to you; it fits you. Your reality satisfies your values, your interests, and your needs. You have a personal and cultural history that differs from those of other people. You express yourself differently from other people, partly as a result of your history and partly as a result of filters derived from your perspective, values, and history. Those filters then influence your perspective, your values, and what you do in the future. Your life moves in a spiral; your past influences your present, and your present influences your future. These influences determine what's important to you—they create what you believe is true, real, good, or beautiful. And, for you, perception *is* reality (as it is for me and for everyone else).

The accompanying box lists the key elements of any person's perspective, or snapshot of reality. When we eavesdrop on May's and Alice's luncheon conversation, see if you can spot what aspects of each person's perspective escalate the discussion into open hostility.

Different Perspectives and Different Realities

May arrives in the cafeteria and waits for Alice for what seems a long time (actually, only five minutes) and is beginning to believe that the other woman won't show up when Alice comes through the cafeteria line. She doesn't seem to have much appetite, either. All she carries to the table is a cup of coffee.

Alice: Sorry I'm late. I had to stop in the rest room for a few minutes.
May: It's okay. It's better that I ate this meager meal before you got here.
Alice: You wanted to talk.

Building Blocks of Realtiy

1. Values
2. Interests
3. Needs
4. Personal history
5. Cultural history
6. Language
7. Attitudes
8. Filters (e.g., bias, feelings, emotions, assumed beliefs)

May: I think we need to.
Alice: What about?
May [*Surprised by Alice's question, she responds in a hissed whisper.*]: Why, what you did yesterday and today.
Alice [*leaning across the table and hissing in return*]: Look. You let me down. So what's there to talk about?
May: I—What do you mean, let you down? Look at the position you put me in. [*May speaks a little louder.*]
Alice: All I asked you to do was to cover for me. What was the big deal? I'd have done the same for you. [*Alice's voice gets a little louder also.*]
May [*recovering and speaking in a hissed whisper*]: I wouldn't ever put you in that position. If I can't come in, I'll talk to Barbara myself. I wouldn't ask you to lie for me.
Alice [*quietly but not in a whisper*]: You don't understand my situation, May. So don't try to put yourself in my shoes. [*Her anger and hurt are clear from her tone of voice.*]
May [*exasperated*]: Why don't you tell me what's going on so I can understand?
Alice: It's none of your business.
May: Alice, since you're dragging me into this, you're making it my business.
Alice [*Drains her cup and stands. She glares at May, and her voice is controlled, almost steely.*]: I've got work to do. You want to fight, but I don't. So buzz off.

[*May sits in stunned silence, watching Alice's back as she stomps angrily out of the door.*]

May: Damn! She even left me her cup to carry to the window.

Well, May didn't want to fight, but that's how it appeared to Alice. Here's a case where two different worlds collided, rather than merged. May didn't recognize that people see and hear the world from different perspectives, have different values and different personal and cultural histories, and express themselves through filters derived from those perspectives, values, and histories. As a result, she thought that Alice should see things the way she did. Alice wanted May to lie, but May couldn't, so she did the best she could. Besides, Alice dumped two big files on her to handle. Alice wasn't being fair or considerate. May didn't intend to fight; she hoped only to settle the matter once and for all.

Alice saw a different reality, one in which she asked May for a simple favor—to tell Barbara anything to cover for her. To Alice, that required more than merely "She can't come in today." As Alice saw it, May was not really lying. She was only embellishing the truth a little, exaggerating. People do it all the time, Alice thought, and this time Alice needed May to do it for her.

Because no two people live in the same world, what you intend and how the other person interprets what you say are different. It's more than that I say "tomayto" and you say "tomahto." It involves a whole system of devices that we use to make the world a comfortable place in which to live, as well as a whole battery of protections that we throw into place whenever we feel threatened. The gap between what you intend and what others perceive is what everyone calls "differences of opinions." This cliché makes the situation sound fairly civil and easy to manage, but, in fact, the differences of opinions that result from these variations in perspectives can harden into battle lines drawn in setting concrete.

May thought she was being reasonable to call for a conversation to settle the matter. To get things started, she verbally flashed her world—her reality as she saw it—onto the table: "what you did yesterday and today." Alice countered with her world—her reality as she saw it: "You let me down."

Then they expanded on their realities. "Look at the position you put me in," May complained. But Alice couldn't see into May's world. "All I asked you to do was to cover for me." That's all that Alice could say and was the reason she asked, "What was the big deal?" The values in her world make her position all the more reasonable to her: "I'd have done the same for you."

These different worlds are constructed out of different filters through which events are seen or heard and interpreted. You can't eliminate filters, but you can manage them through a better conceived discussion than the one May created. Constructive confrontation requires planning to be successful, and it requires a climate in which the confrontation can effectively merge two different realities into one perception that satisfies the interests of both parties to the conflict.

Setting the Climate

May and Alice have had an amicable relationship up to this point, but they can't be considered friends. They don't know each other all that well, they haven't shared many experiences or exchanged deep personal values or concerns. As a result, the climate in which they work is one amenable to superficial exchanges and rituals, but not to managing conflict.

Constructive confrontation is most effective

when the conditions for it are right. A climate of trust and caring must exist. The conditions for May and Alice were totally wrong: (1) Their past relationship didn't encourage this type of discussion; (2) the setting was wrong—too public; (3) the timing was wrong—a forty-five-minute lunch break doesn't provide enough opportunity to air real differences and to manage them; (4) the agenda was vague and ambiguous ("Let's talk"); (5) the atmosphere was charged with accusation—what Alice did and what May didn't do. At least Alice didn't leave May with the bill, as well as the dirty cup.

Relationships: Two people who barely know each other need to attack the issues that separate them differently from two people who know each other well. Trust and caring are missing from most working acquaintanceships. Although we talk about "trusting you until you earn my distrust," we usually don't really trust strangers or acquaintances. We're taught as children to distrust one another ("Never talk to strangers.")

This doesn't mean that you can't create a climate of trust and caring, even if you don't make everyone your friend. Taking every opportunity for talking with people and getting past the daily ceremonial exchanges ("How you doing?" "Fine. How you doing?" "Fine.") takes a little effort and a willingness to disclose your feelings and thoughts, but it can prevent conflicts from occurring in the first place or lead to a climate in which conflicts can be resolved.

Being honest and candid lets people know what you feel, what you like and don't like, what you value and don't value. Doing things to help others be more successful at what they do and lending a hand when someone needs assistance establish your reliability and credibility. Then, when you say, "I'd like to talk about how I feel about what happened yesterday," other people will be willing to listen, and they might even pay attention.

Setting: You can handle delicate issues effectively only if you have privacy. You need a conference room or an empty office—a place with a door that can close out curious stares from other people and block sounds from reaching their ears. It's difficult, if not impossible, to bare your soul when everyone's listening—especially if you're being forced to whisper when you want to yell.

Timing: You not only need time in which to resolve the conflict, you have to pick the right time as well as the right place. Alice and May might have been better off meeting after work, alone to talk openly. They could have made arrangements to stay as late as they needed to, which might have meant meeting on a different day.

Postponing the conversation until later in the day or until the next day might have also allowed them to distance themselves from their feelings. You're not avoiding the problem as long as you ensure that, when you do get together, all the relevant and important issues are confronted.

The Agenda: To ensure that you get all the relevant and important issues on to the table, you need to set an agenda. Compare "Let's talk" with "I'd like to talk about how I feel about what happened yesterday. Because I have a problem with doing what you asked me to do, I'd like us to work out an equitable way of handling similar situations in the future." Okay, so it's wordier, but it's a complete agenda. And that's what you need in order to resolve a conflict.

The Atmosphere: May opened the conversation by accusing Alice: "what you did yesterday and today." That not only charged Alice with wrongdoing (which Alice doesn't believe she is guilty of), it also charged the atmosphere negatively. The wordier agenda in the previous paragraph creates a positive charge without accusing anyone of anything. The agenda says, "I want to talk about how I feel (not about what you did). I want to talk about my problem (not your asking me to lie). I want to work out a plan that satisfies both our needs (not my insistence that you never ask me to lie again)." Such a climate promotes understanding and problem solving: constructive confrontation.

Think about your own workplace. What has anyone there done to create a climate in which people can work together to resolve differences of opinion before the differences become conflicts? What has anyone there done to make it possible to resolve conflicts when they do arise? If no one has done anything along these lines yet, you may become reactive, rather than proactive, when you experience a potential conflict. Waiting for something bad to happen without doing anything to prevent it is like waiting for a fatal accident before installing a traffic signal at a dangerous intersection.

CHAPTER FOUR

Giving Feedback

Saying to someone, "You're a liar, and I'm not" could get you punched in the nose—even if (especially if) it's true. Although it may be open and candid feedback, which you need for effective constructive confrontation, a statement such as "You're a liar, and I'm not" isn't effective communication. Several other conditions, in addition to favorable timing, place, and climate, have to be established before you can use feedback to help merge perspectives and resolve conflicts.

Positioning Feedback

Feedback tells people how their behavior affects you—what it did and how you feel about it. It can also ask people to change their behavior in order to prevent negative results from recurring. And complete feedback includes a reference to consequences—what might happen if the behavior changes and what might happen if it doesn't.

Instead of, "You're a liar, and I'm not," you could say, "I know that what you said isn't true; therefore, I can't repeat it because it makes me feel terrible to say things I know aren't true." Yes, that's also wordier than the first way, and yes, people don't usually talk that way, which is probably why people get into fights they'd rather not have. How would you rather have it—sound rather long-winded or get punched in the nose?

In May's case, she could have said, "Please don't ask me to do what you asked of me again. If we don't work out some accommodation to each other's needs, we'll be at each other's throats all the time. I'd rather we have a good working relationship. What do you think we can do to resolve this?" That's what May could have said, but she didn't. As a result, Alice got up and walked out, feeling indignant.

You really needn't talk funny to give effective feedback, but you do have to meet certain conditions in order to be effective.

Assessing Readiness

Most people don't ask for feedback, although they probably should. Yet, in most instances, if properly approached, people are willing to listen to your reactions to what they do and say. They must be willing to listen, or you'll end up talking *at* them, rather than *with* them. If you have teenaged children, you know exactly what I mean.

May tried to salvage the discussion when she went back upstairs to the claims area.

May: Apparently you don't want to talk about the same things I do, and you don't want to talk about them now. I'd like another crack at resolving this. What do you suggest we do?

Alice [*looking up for just a moment and shaking her head*]: Let's let it lie for now, May. I'll let you know when I'm ready.

May: Will you really do that?

Alice: Yes. I will. I won't forget because I need to get something out of this, too.

Meeting Needs: People are more receptive to feedback if they see that it will meet their needs. Alice and May are probably not talking about meeting the same needs, but Alice has let May know that she'll accept May's feedback only if there's something in it for her. Unless the feedback can meet her needs, she'll see it as worthless.

At the same time, you have to recognize your rights, as well. As I said in Chapter 2, constructive confrontation is assertive. When you confront someone in this manner, you recognize both your rights and the other person's. Neither of you has to roll over and play dead—which is a lose-lose situation all the way around.

Ensuring Accuracy: Did Alice actually ask May to lie? She did say, "Make up something creative, would you? I can't even think straight today." But does that mean "lie"? Alice doesn't think so, even if May does.

If May had asked Alice exactly what she meant by "make up something creative," Alice might have answered, "I really didn't mean anything by it. Maybe you could have said, 'She sounded terrible. Bad enough that she didn't want to talk to me about it. Something private. Said she couldn't think straight.' " Because May didn't ask, both May and Alice are talking about lying, but they're not talking about the same thing. In short, check out the accuracy of your perceptions to prevent misdirected discussions that could produce bad feelings.

Involving the Other Person: You're both locked in the fray when you're in conflict with each other. If the other person is trampling on your needs, it's because she has needs to meet, also. Therefore, if you both participate in coming up with a solution to the problem, the chances are the solution you adopt will be mutually satisfying. If you give the other person the option of taking corrective action or doing nothing at all, you are offering to share responsibility. You create a win-win, mutually satisfying result.

May and Alice are far from this stage. They still haven't gotten past mutual accusations of mistreatment. They're in confrontation, but they're not engaged in problem solving.

Accepting Feedback: Other people will be more receptive to feedback from you if they know that you're also willing to accept feedback. If you become defensive or argumentative, you step across the line from constructive to destructive confrontation. "What do you mean, let you down? Look at the position you put me in," May said. Her reaction was both defensive and attacking, which merely escalated the situation.

What do you think Alice would have said if May had responded differently? Maybe she would have said, "I don't understand. If you'll clarify how you see the situation, we can deal with it better." It's one thing to seek clarification, another to join in an attack.

To deal with the other person's perspective, it's important to know how she feels about the situation, about what you're saying, and about what you want from her. You can't really know any of that unless you ask for feedback. Again, May could have said, "I really don't know how I let you down. Please explain it." She could have asked for that feedback, but she didn't. Instead, she considered the best defense to be an offense, the result of which was Alice's similar but stronger reaction.

Using I-Statements

May and Alice could have taken a lot of the sting out of their approach to one another if they had been less accusatory. Combine their verbal attacks with a jabbing index finger and you're bordering on what, in some states' criminal codes, is called fighting words, which can be a defense against a charge of assault.

I-statements give feedback the substance it's supposed to have. In addition, since feedback is a report about how something has affected you, using I-statements when giving feedback prevents many of the barriers to conflict resolution. Here's another example of what May could have said.

May: When you called yesterday and asked me to talk to Barbara for you and to handle your files, I felt very put upon. I thought, rightly or wrongly, that you were putting me in a position of having to lie to Barbara; I also felt overloaded by having to take on your files. I'd like to work out an arrangement whereby it won't happen again, or I'm going to ask for a conference with Barbara.

I-statements, like the one May could have used, have four parts. You can take them in whatever order makes sense at the time, but you should separate them from each other to make sure you make yourself perfectly clear. These elements are listed in the box. Analyze the I-statements I just proposed for May to see how they reflect these elements.

Four Parts to an Effective I-Statement

1. What you experienced or what you perceived.
2. What you felt about your experience (what you liked or didn't like), and why.
3. What you would like to see happen differently in the future (what you need from the other person).
4. The consequences you see if things don't change.

Using I-Statements to Give Feedback: I-statements guide your feedback to the proper targets: behaviors, feelings, and desired results. However, to use I-statements effectively, you have to aim them properly. Emphasize what you see, hear, and feel, rather than what the other person does or says, and explain how your reaction affects you or how you perform a task. Here are six basic guidelines for making your feedback more effective:

1. Use action verbs, rather than a form of the verb "to be." Say, "When you called," "I thought," "I felt," "I'd like to work out," instead of, "You are."
2. Avoid labeling people or making accusations. Say, "I thought you were asking me to lie," rather than, "You're a liar."
3. When talking about what someone did, deal with observables; describe behaviors

over which the other person has some control. Say, "You asked me to take on two very difficult files. I felt overloaded," instead of, "You're a lazy shirker."
4. Be specific and respond to a situation as soon after it affects you as you can; delay or create distance only if the other person is too distracted or distressed to listen to or benefit from feedback.
5. Be honest and direct, dealing with those matters that directly affect you and about which you have personal knowledge, but don't be brutal and uncaring.
6. Spell out the consequences of not doing anything about the situation.

Giving feedback makes your position, your feelings or emotions, and your reasoning explicit. It helps people understand what's important to you and gives others a glimpse of what your reality looks like to you. At the same time, the feedback you give has to consider the other person's needs and feelings. To quote my favorite Native American proverb, "To give a person dignity is above all things."

CHAPTER FIVE

Listening to Feedback

෴

Tell the truth, be open, be candid, give feedback. That's all fine advice, but if you stop there, nothing will happen to make life between you and the person with whom you're in conflict any better. To make a discussion effective, you need to encourage other people to express themselves (or to think out loud, if they haven't formulated a clear and concise position). You have to encourage them to explore your viewpoint, to make sure they understand what you're saying, and, perhaps, to find points on which they might take issue with you.

Letting people explore your position also helps you clarify your own perceptions, uncovering correct, as well as erroneous, assumptions. Not only might May, in Chapter 4, have explored Alice's views, she might have asked Alice to explore her view as well. Perhaps she could have asked, "Alice, what do you think has me so upset?" In effect, this question asks for feedback.

Encouraging others to provide different viewpoints (including their assumptions) converts a confrontational discussion into a dialogue. Whereas a discussion limits you to an exchange of ideas, a dialogue goes beyond persuading the other person to accept your opinion, examining fundamental assumptions, values, and attitudes and seeking out new or different mutually satisfying possibilities for action. But to make dialogue work for you, you need to listen to what the other person is saying. No, not hear—listen.

Ineffective Listening

Talking about your perceptions or feelings is one-half of the equation; the ability to listen well is the other half. Active listening—participating in the other person's conversation without diverting it to other topics or to yourself—is the most effective method of communicating. May and Alice don't know how to do this.

They have another try at reconciliation the next evening after work. But it doesn't work out too well. See if you can spot why it doesn't.

Alice: So. Now what?

May: I think you don't understand what I'm trying to tell you.

Alice: Tell me again.

May: I can't lie to Barbara for anyone, not even for myself.

Alice: So, who asked you to lie?

May: You did.

Alice: No, I didn't. I just wanted you to tell her I wasn't coming in, but in a way that would make her understand that I wasn't just shirking.

May [*insists on placing the blame on Alice*]: How about dumping those tough files on me?

Alice: I didn't think they were so tough. I had done the investigation. My notes were clear, and you didn't have to do much more than relay messages.

May: They couldn't be put off, and I had to do some strong talking and a little arm twisting on both of them.

Alice: That's why they pay us the big bucks—to handle these tough cases. You're just as good at it as I am. Better, maybe. So what's the beef?

May: It was your responsibility to call Barbara and your responsibility to close those files.

Alice: I know that, but I had some problems at home that took a very high priority. Unless I handled them, I wouldn't have been able to come in yesterday, either. Maybe not even today. Then what?

May: You're going to have to work out something to take care of your personal needs on your own time.

Alice: May, let's stop this here. I'm just getting as angry with you as you seem to be with me. I'm going home.

Does this discussion seem familiar? Have you ever found yourself locked in this sort of going-nowhere, tell-them-nothing, negatively charged exchange of air? And May had so many openings for changing the tone of the whole discussion and working out a fair and reasonable accommodation—all of which escaped her.

Active Listening

Active listening is the most effective method for understanding what a person says to you. Everything people say has both a content element (i.e., what the person is talking about) and an expressive element (i.e., how the person feels about what he or she is saying). You can understand both what the speaker means and what he or she feels about it only if you give the person a chance to explain and help by probing or giving appropriate feedback. That's active listening.

Appropriate Feedback: Dialogue is based on two speakers' understanding of each other's perspective. When those perspectives are clearly defined, both people can identify points at which the perspectives overlap, as well as points at which they butt up against each other. Two devices, special forms of the feedback I described in Chapter 4, will help you develop active listening skills. They are called informational feedback and reflective feedback and are defined in the box.

Informational and Reflective Feedback

1. *Informational feedback*: Paraphrasing, telling the other person what you think he said. This kind of feedback helps you grasp the content of what the other person has said—his verbal communication.
2. *Reflective feedback*: Acknowledging signals you receive from the other person about how she feels about what she's saying. This kind of feedback helps you grasp the expressive element—usually nonverbal—in what the other person has said.

How differently the conversation might have gone had Alice reacted differently when May said, "I can't lie to Barbara for anyone, not even for myself."

"Oh," Alice might have responded. "If I understand what you're saying, you think I wanted you to lie" (informational feedback). "And that has you pretty upset" (reflective feedback).

May had her opening when Alice said, "I just wanted you to tell her I wasn't coming in but in a way that would make her understand that I wasn't just shirking."

"Then you meant something different from what I understood you to say," May might have responded (informational feedback).

Then they would have been in a position to

engage in a dialogue about what Alice meant and how May feels about it.

Probing: Alice obviously did not volunteer much information. Therefore, May had no way of understanding what Alice meant when she said, "I had some problems at home that took a very high priority. Unless I handled them, I wouldn't have been able to come in yesterday, either. Maybe not even today. Then what?"

We've been taught not to ask questions about personal matters. We become very uncomfortable when coworkers voluntarily confide personal things, and probing about them creates great discomfort. May did what most people would do when Alice opened up the door to her realities just a crack; she slammed it shut again herself. As a result, Alice took the opportunity to avoid dealing with the issues again.

You don't have to be a busybody when probing. May could have asked for clarification several times during the conversation. For example, she might have asked, "Then what did you mean when you asked me to be creative?" or "How do you think I should react when you ask me to take over your files?" Answers to such questions lay a foundation for reconciling differences and for resolving conflicts.

The personal issue posed a difficult judgment call for May. How far should she have pushed for information? When Alice mentioned her personal problems, May's probe could have been something like, "That sounds serious." How much Alice chose to volunteer would have been her decision. She could have said nothing more than, "It is," to which May could have responded, "Serious enough to cause you to miss work again—say, within the next few days or weeks?"

Alice might have responded, "It could. Please understand, I wouldn't be asking for your help if it weren't this serious." On the other hand, Alice might have been willing to volunteer more information. Since May didn't do any probing at all, however, Alice didn't have to volunteer any information at all.

Other Devices That Communicate: To help other people explain themselves, you can use other active listening devices, most of which are nonverbal signals that tell people you're really interested in what they have to say.

Verbals are the words you use. However, it's the nonverbal signals—including tone of voice, gestures, facial expressions, and body language—that communcuate over 90 percent of what you mean, as well as what you feel and think. When you are listening actively, how you signal to another person, verbally and nonverbally, either encourages that person to talk to you or discourages her.

Some nonverbals (e.g., murmuring "Hmm" or nodding), as well as verbals (e.g., saying "I see") encourage people to continue talking; other nonverbals (e.g., folding your arms across your chest), more than verbals, discourage people from talking.

Both nonverbals (e.g., smiling) and verbals (e.g., "I understand") make your understanding and your feelings known.

May and Alice may never get their problems resolved because, even though they're talking with each other, they're not communicating. No, communication hasn't broken down. That's an inaccurate description. Either you communicate or you don't. Communication takes place only when both you and the other person understand each other and reach closure about what you both are saying and feeling. You don't have to agree on the outcome. Alice doesn't have to say, "I'll never do it again." Rather, to communicate effectively, you have to understand and agree on the issues that you have discussed.

Alice: I understand your point, May. You felt that I took advantage of you and asked you to do things you couldn't in good conscience do.

May: I understand yours, too, Alice. You had some serious personal matters that kept you from coming to work, and you needed my help.

Now, if they had reached these points of closure, May and Alice would have been communicating. But they haven't reached them; therefore, they need help, they need a mediator, and they turn to Barbara for help. Read on.

CHAPTER SIX

Mediating Between Warring Factions

∽

When two or more people around you are at war, keeping your distance may seem to be your best option. But, in some situations, staying out of the conflict may result in a lose-lose outcome that causes you as much pain as it does the combatants. In other situations, you can't remain above the fray because, as in Barbara's case, it's part of your job to get into it when you're needed. However, there are ways to get into it, and there are ways to get into it—wrong ways and right ways.

One wrong way to mediate is to jump into the situation when it doesn't concern you at all and no one has asked you to help. If you do, chances are the two people will find a common enemy against whom they can unite—you. Other possibilities are that one person will attempt to pit you against the other and that both of them will try to drag you into a pit. Either way, it's a no-win situation for you.

Another wrong way is to take sides, even if one side or the other is flagrantly at fault. Mediators have to remain neutral, impartial, and unbiased. When you lean to one side, the other side will see it and either turn against you or double efforts to change your mind. Alternatively, the person toward whom you are leaning may try to take advantage of the sympathetic ear you provide. Again, either way, you lose.

A good rule of thumb comes from the title of an old song: "Fools rush in where angels fear to tread." There is a time and a way to mediate a dispute when combatants reach an impasse.

Timing Your Intervention

Timing is everything when trying to mediate a dispute. Intervening too soon can upset the conflict resolution process; intervening too late can make the conflict permanent and irreconcilable.

Intervening on invitation is an excellent tactic. Intervening when the people in conflict reach an impasse is a necessary tactic.

Take this assumption as a self-evident truth. You can't resolve a conflict between two other people. Only they can do it. All you can do is help them manage the situation more effectively. If you think this way, you'll be able to stay apart from the situation until you're asked to come in.

You can solicit an invitation—as long as you're not too eager to intervene. If the others sense that you're more interested in solving the problem than they are, they'll place the burden of the effort on your shoulders. You'll wind up with the mess in your hands, instead of in theirs, where it belongs.

Barbara, May's and Alice's boss, wasn't aware of what was happening until she noticed a definite chill between the two women as they worked together on a project she assigned to them. Even though they were to complete a report for her and present it as a team, they worked separately and hardly spoke to each as they did their research and prepared the report. At the meeting in which they made their presentation, it was as if they had two separate reports to deliver.

May's and Alice's presentations were adequate. All the information was there, but the presentation was far from inspiring. When they were finished, Barbara thanked them for their effort.

Barbara: I noticed some redundancy between what you two did. Didn't you work on this together?
May: Some. [*Alice nods in agreement.*]
Barbara: It doesn't seem as if you did.
May: Well, we didn't write the report together.

> [*Barbara spots Alice's hostile glance in May's direction and notes the hostility in May's voice.*]

Barbara: Might I ask you two what's going on? [*May and Alice glance at one another, but neither answers.*] Well, okay, but if you need me, you know where to find me.

> [*On the way back to their cubicles, May reaches out and takes Alice's arm.*]

May: What do you think? Should we ask her for help working this out?
Alice [*sulkily*]: Do as you wish.
May: Don't you think we can use a mediator here?
Alice: Okay. What do you want to do?
May [*turns back toward Barbara's office*]: Now?
Alice [*smiles*]: Sure. Why not?

But what if May and Alice hadn't come back? What if the conflict had continued unabated? Then Barbara would have had to step in and be a bit more direct and forceful—because their conflict was having a negative effect on their work. Unabated, the dispute could have had a negative effect on the morale of the group, as well as on May and Alice. Or it could have had a negative effect on other work-related factors. These are all good reasons for intervention.

Your motivation for intervening has to come from some productive source. "Doing good" is usually valued only by the "good doer." As I noted earlier, stepping in uninvited can result in a lose-lose situation for you, as well as for the other people. On the other hand, you should step in if the conflict affects you, your work, or the work of other people for whom you're responsible. Then the outcome *is* your responsibility.

The Mediator's Role

Unlike the referee in a boxing match, an effective mediator is not in the middle of the situation. Instead, like a judge ringside, she stays apart, with a clear view of the whole ring. Yet, like a referee, she separates the people sparring with each other and leads them into new directions when it seems that they can't break out of their own clinches. She listens, she examines the data, she seeks out the common ground; she looks for new or additional information and summarizes. She makes decisions only if the situation becomes desperate—when it seems as if the fighters will knock each other out unless she declares an end to the fight.

Listening: Active listening is a mediator's most important tool.

Barbara: Tell me what's happening.
Alice: I asked May to cover for me one day when I couldn't come in. She thought I asked her to lie for me, and she's been angry at me ever since. I've been angry with her because, when you talked with me about my absence, it seemed that she told you I was merely shirking. But I had my reasons for missing work.
Barbara: May?
May: It's a little more than that. She had these two files to close, and. . . .

We don't have to go over all the old ground again, but notice how Barbara elicited the information she needed. She could have taken one of several common but misguided approaches, including giving a lecture about teamwork and making threats of serious consequences if they didn't get together. Instead, she used just two simple probes. She might ask a few more questions to get more information, but her main job is to listen rather than to talk.

Examining: A second function of the mediator is to examine, to look at the situation with a critical eye. Some informational feedback helps.

Barbara: So let me get this straight. From your point of view, Alice, May's report to me did more harm than good. From your perspective, May, Alice took advantage of you and expected you to fabricate a story. Is that right?

When both of them agreed that Barbara had a grasp of the situation, Barbara asked Alice, "What did you want May to say or do?" She later asked May, "What would have been more appropriate for you?" She asked questions that not only helped Barbara understand what had been happening but also helped Alice and May sort out the experience into a concise, clear picture. Shining a light on the facts makes them easier for everyone to see.

Looking for Common Ground: As long as May and Alice stay within their own views of the world, surrounding themselves with their own realities, they'll circle a midpoint in parallel orbits that never converge. It's Barbara's job as mediator to help them find shared realities, issues on which they can both agree without feeling beaten or defeated.

A good place to start the search for a solution is to have the disputants agree on a specific, concisely worded outcome they want from the negotiations.

Barbara: What do you two hope to accomplish by coming in here to work this out?

May [*jumps at the opportunity to repeat her wish*]: I'd like to see us agree on how to handle situations like this in the future.

Barbara: Situations like what?

May: You know. If Alice can't make it in, we have a way to handle who says what to whom and who does what with the files.

Barbara: Okay. That's what you want. Alice?

Alice: I just want—I really don't know what I want. I just don't like the anger around here. I've got enough in my life to contend with right now without coming here for more of the same.

Looking for New or Additional Data or Information: Alice has raised a red flag. It wouldn't do, at this point, for Barbara to insist that Alice declare a personal objective for the discussion. Before she can help May and Alice reach a common ground, she has to chase after what Alice just said. Here's where appropriate probing helps to get at new information that can change everyone's view of the situation.

Both Barbara and May wait for Alice to go on. Silence is something like a vacuum, and, as you probably learned in high school, nature abhors a vacuum. Since the silence is deliberate, it's pregnant with expectation. Someone has to fill the silence, which is, in itself, a probe. Under these circumstances, the person for whom everyone is waiting is the one who speaks first (or should speak first).

Alice: I have some problems at home. I try to keep them separate—home and here—but sometimes home gets in the way of here whether I want it to or not.

Barbara: I see.

Alice [*in a flat, emotionless voice*]: It's my husband. He has a drinking problem. I probably drink a little too much myself, but only at home, and I'm never drunk. He gets drunk, and sometimes he gets violent. The morning I couldn't come in, I was in a lot of pain. He had knocked me down, and my hip and back were bruised. [*Alice stops, takes a deep breath, and averts her eyes.*] I put him out of the house over the weekend and took my case to an attorney. I guess I've been somewhat distracted by all this.

May: I wish you had told me.

Alice: It's my burden, not yours.

May: I could have been more understanding.

Alice [*looks at Barbara*]: I guess that's my goal. Understanding. Not sympathy, May. I've gotten things under control, but I am going through a difficult time. The more I get it all straightened out, the easier it's becoming to get back on track.

Barbara: I think I see what we have here.

Summarizing: This role is crucial to success. It's the basis for further discussion, problem solving, and action planning. After Barbara spells out both sides as she sees them, she offers May and Alice a goal statement on which she believes they both can agree.

Barbara: So, Alice, you may or may not have a few more difficult days and may or may not need help handling your files. And you, May, you want to help Alice when you can, but you want to work out a system everyone agrees is fair. Do I have all this right?

Not all disputes are as easy as this one to resolve, and even this one isn't completely settled. They have yet to work out an action plan that will satisfy everyone. Here, once more, the mediator has to step outside the ring to let the people engaged in the struggle decide what's best for them. This is the moment at which you have to bite your tongue lest you make suggestions, because, if your ideas don't work, guess who'll get blamed for stirring up the mess?

CHAPTER SEVEN

Taking Action

At the heart of all conflicts there resides at least one problem that must be solved. If you feel that someone is obstructing your ability and your right to satisfy your needs, you have to start with identifying what is producing the blockage before you can give accurate feedback about it or take action on it. If you're a supervisor, you have an interest in the solution if the obstacle is preventing you from meeting your work's objectives or your unit's goals.

In our story, Alice must maintain her file closing rates, which is necessary for maintaining the unit's productivity objectives. Failure to do so could jeopardize Alice's appraisal to her detriment. Shifting Alice's work load to May could swamp May and throw her behind, jeopardizing her appraisal to her detriment. If everyone falls behind, Barbara's numbers will look bad and affect other units, such as accounts payable and data processing. Not only does attention have to be paid, action also must be taken.

Action Planning
Arriving at a mutual understanding on what is causing the differences of opinion or values involved in the conflict may not be sufficient to resolve the conflict. Agreeing on the nature of the problem demands that both parties hammer out a

mutually satisfying action plan for preventing a similar occurrence in the future. That plan embodies the solution of the problem, but it's worthless if it's not executed as quickly as possible.

The Need for a Jointly Created Plan

You've seen what happens when the National Labor Relations Board or a court hands down a plan to parties in conflict. Since the disputants didn't produce the plan, they feel no obligation to execute it; whatever they do, they do from fear of legal consequences, rather than from a common desire to see justice done for the benefit of all.

One objective of conflict resolution is the elimination of antagonism and the adversarial nature of the relationship between the parties in the conflict. The conversion of bad feelings into a merged view of the situation requires cooperation and a common objective. It's necessary that both people involved in the conflict agree on a desirable outcome of the dispute in order to change parallel orbits into overlapping circles. That overlap represents the convergence of realities that both share and enables both parties to produce a jointly proposed action plan.

Problem Solving

Handing down a solution may become necessary if you're a mediator, but only when a stand-off between the opponents makes jointly created action impossible. Properly executed problem solving prevents that kind of impasse.

Too often, people leap at hasty conclusions, confusing the symptoms of a problem with its solution. You may be able to relieve the pain of a broken bone with codeine, but that won't help mend the break. The eight steps listed in the box on the next page facilitate the problem-solving and decision-making process.

Collect Data and Formulate an Initial Statement of the Problem: When you know what should be or what you expect from each other, you can compare that goal with what is actually happening. You can build a picture of reality on which you both can agree, creating the common ground from which a solution can be reached.

Alice: Ideally, I'll not need that kind of help again. But, in the event I do, the ideal then is that I call Barbara, not you, May, and be up-front with her. She can decide what to do with my work load.

May: I agree.

Barbara [*nodding*]: That's really how it should be.

Alice: I know that's not what happened. Calling you, May, shifted the burden of responsibility from me to you, and that's what caused most of the difficulty.

May: That's true. Ideally, I shouldn't have to do that. The fact that I did take it on myself even though I knew that I shouldn't have made me feel even worse. I guess we collaborated on what happened. It was as much my fault as yours.

Examine the Contributing Factors: Once you know what actually happened that generated the conflict, you need to look at the whole picture.

Steps to Take to Solve Problems

1. Collect data comparing what should be or what you expect from each other with what has actually happened.
2. Express the initial statement of the problem as an unfavorable relationship between what you expect from each other and what has actually happened.
3. Identify contributing factors and specify how they contribute to the problem.
4. Express the final statement of the problem as a relationship between contributing factors and expectations, desires, or needs; include the consequences of not correcting the situation.
5. Identify steps both of you will take to prevent those contributing factors from occurring again.
6. Identify benefits from the plan for both parties.
7. Identify a time for sitting down to discuss your relationship again.
8. Identify a means for communicating any problems that arise in the future.

What happened is not the cause; it's the effect. Why did the problem occur? Who was involved? How often does it happen? When and under what circumstances does it happen? Where does it happen?

Barbara: Why did you get so upset, May?
May: I misunderstood what Alice wanted. I thought she was asking me to lie. Whenever someone expects me to do that, I get upset. Wouldn't you?
Barbara: So Alice asked you to relay a message but didn't give you explicit instructions.
May: That's right.
Barbara: In the absence of those instructions, you read into the request a demand that you lie to me.
May: Exactly.
Barbara: Alice, what does that tell you?
Alice: Like I said, I should've talked directly to you. But I see what really went wrong. You know, it happens to me more than I like to admit. I don't usually realize it until after the fact that I'm too cryptic—sometimes too flippant.

Now the realities are merging. The participants' total worlds are still separate, but where they're in touch, instead of butting up against each other, they blend into a common picture.

Formulate the Final Statement of the Problem:
The common picture is the problem to be solved before the conflict can be set permanently to rest.

Barbara: Maybe you two need to summarize the situation—pull together all the pieces we've uncovered here. I'll write down what you say, and we can use that

	statement as a guide for further discussion. Take a few minutes to talk it over. Make this a joint communique, as they say in international circles.
Alice	[*taking a pad of paper from Barbara's desk*]: I think we'll need this.
	[*She and May huddle, chat, and scribble notes while Barbara busies herself with other things. It takes longer than a few minutes, but, by the time they are finished, they can read the statement to their supervisor.*]
Alice:	The real problem is that neither of us should ever expect the other to take responsibility for each other's work or work requirements. Instead, we should assume responsibility only for ourselves. However, when we do need help from one another, we need to be specific, clear, cooperative, and supportive.

A common reality is clearly identified by the use of the word we. It's "our world" rather than "my world" and "your world."

Map Out Steps for Taking Corrective Action: Good intentions by themselves get you nowhere. To resolve a conflict successfully, you have to identify *doable* steps both of you will take to prevent contributing factors from happening again. The steps have to be specific, realistic, and achievable within a given period of time.

Alice:	I think this whole situation I'm in will take care of itself very soon—within a month. I've gotten a restraining order on my husband. He pledges to obey it.

	He's also remorseful now and promises to seek help. So I may not need you to help me that way again.
Barbara:	Do you think that's what you really need to work on?
Alice:	Well, it'll help. But you're right. My first goal has to be not to be late or absent again. Second, I need to face you, rather than pass the ball to May. All that has to start immediately. I'll call you if I need to do something outside of work.
May:	And I need to be more supportive. No, that's not exactly right. I need to suspend my personal judgment before jumping to conclusions. I should have asked you immediately what you meant by "be creative." I could have saved us all a lot of grief. So, in the future, my goal is to insist that you be specific.

Identify Benefits: The outcome of negotiating the resolution of a conflict has to be more than a mere detente. "Live and let live" is less than a solution. Everyone needs to get something from the plan for it to work; there has to be a mutual benefit.

May:	I'll not only be happier with what you're asking me to do, it'll make it easier for you to ask a favor of me.
Alice:	I'll probably save myself a lot of grief with other people as well as with you, May, if I work at this. I owe you an apology, too, Barbara. I admit it. I didn't trust you to understand what

I'm going through. But you do. You both do, and I appreciate it very much.

Monitor the Relationship: Setting time frames helps you to identify a time for sitting down to discuss your relationship again. Time limits become milestones for measuring how effective you are in executing your plan. A mechanism for communicating any problems with how things are going has to be attached to the plan as well.

May: I'll give you immediate feedback if I think you're not communicating with me as effectively as you can.
Alice: Thanks. I think we need to give each other more feedback than that. Review how we're doing, how we're getting along. At least once. A week from today? What do you think, Barbara?
Barbara: How does that sound to the two of you?
May: I think it's a good idea.
Alice: Yeah. I think it's necessary.
Barbara: Then I agree. Do you think you'll need me in your session?
Alice: No.
May: I think we've got it under control. We have all these notes that will help us work it out, track it, and talk it over.
Alice: Thanks for your help, Barbara.
May: Yes. Thank you very much.

Did they all live happily ever after? Well, happily ever after may be too strong, but they were *happier.* That was May and Alice's critical indicator of success. What more could they have asked for?

Conclusion

Resolving conflicts takes an effort on everyone's part and depends on everyone's willingness to use constructive confrontation, rather than using confrontation as a means for dominating. Everyone also has to rely on personal power rather than status power, even supervisors who have the status power to dominate the situation and other people.

When May and Alice couldn't find the means to satisfy their own needs, they turned to their boss, Barbara, for help. She could have ordered her employees to stop bickering and get back to work or to accept a plan she created for ending the spat. Instead, she used her influence to help them work through a sticky problem.

Regardless of the nature of the conflict, all conflicts involve differences of opinions, values, goals, or desires. Still, not all differences produce, or need to produce, conflict. Whether ordinary differences produce conflict depends in large part on whether they are managed creatively and in a way that is healthy for everyone.

The healthy way to manage most conflicts or potential conflicts includes using constructive confrontation, effective communication techniques, effective problem solving methods, and an effective action plan. These methods will also help you keep ordinary disagreements or differences of opinion or of values from erupting into conflict.

Suggested Readings

֍

Berne, Eric. *Games People Play.* New York: Grove Press, 1964.

Covey, Stephen R. *The Seven Habits of Highly Effective People: Powerful Lessons in Personal Change.* New York: Simon & Schuster, 1989.

Dinksmeyer, Don, and Lewis E. Losoncy. *The Encouragement Book: Becoming a Positive Person.* Englewood Cliffs, N.J.: Prentice-Hall, 1980.

Hill, Norman C. *Increasing Managerial Effectiveness: Keys to Management and Motivation.* Reading, Mass.: Addison-Wesley, 1979.

Robbins, Stephen P. *Managing Organizational Conflict: A Nontraditional Approach.* Englewood Cliffs, N.J.: Prentice-Hall, 1974.

Weiss, Donald H. *How to Deal With Difficult People.* New York: AMACOM, 1987.

———. *How to Get the Best Out of Other People.* New York: AMACOM, 1988.

———. *Managing Conflict,* Rev. ed. Watertown, Mass.: American Management Association, Extension Institute, 1992.

Index

action plan, 44–51
   jointly created, 45
   problem solving as, 45–51
active listening, 29, 31–35, 39–40
agenda for communication, 20–21
aggressiveness, 9
assertiveness, 12
atmosphere for communication, 21
avoidance, 10

body language, 34–35

communication, 13–21
   climate for, 18–21
   differing realities and, 15–18
compromise, 10–11
conflict resolution, 2, 52, *see also* action plan; communication; constructive confrontation; feedback; mediation
conflicts, 2–7
   disagreements vs., 3–7
   values and, 1–2, 14
constructive confrontation, 8–13
   avoidance of, 10
   climate for, 18–21
   compromise vs., 10–11
   confrontation for dominance vs., 9–10
   problem solving through, 11–13
cooperation, 13

disagreements, 3–4
    change from, to conflict, 4–7
domination, confrontation for, 9–10

feedback, 22–35
    accepting, 25–26
    active listening to, 29, 31–35
    assessing readiness for, 23–26
    encouraging, 28–29
    ineffective listening to, 29–31
    I-statements for giving, 26–28
    positioning, 22–23

informational feedback, 31, 32, 40
I-statements, 26–28

listening
    active, 29, 31–35
    ineffective, 29–31
    mediation and, 39–40

mediation, 35–43
    mediator's role in, 39–43
    timing of, 36–39

nonverbal signals, 34–35

probing, 33–34, 41–43
problem solving, 45–51
    benefits of, 50–51
    collecting data for, 46
    constructive confrontation for, 11–13
    corrective action as, 49–50
    factors contributing to conflicts, 46, 48
    monitoring relationships in, 51
    problem statement for, 46, 48–49
    steps for, 47

reality
    building blocks of, 15
    differing perceptions of, 14, 15–18
    shared, 40–41
reflective feedback, 31, 32
relationships
    communication in, 19–20
    monitoring, for problem solving, 51

setting, communication and, 20
status power, 9–10

timing
    for best communication, 20
    of mediation, 36–39

values and conflict, 1–2, 14

About the Author

Donald H. Weiss, Ph.D., is CEO of Self-Management Communications, Inc., St. Louis, and a well-known author of books, videos, and cassette-workbook programs that focus on management and interpersonal skills. He has been a senior training and development executive and consultant for more than twenty-five years. Among his corporate positions were: program manager for the Citicorp Executive Development Center and corporate training manager for Millers' Mutual Insurance. His many publications include fifteen previous books in the SOS series and *Fair, Square, and Legal: Safe Hiring, Managing, and Firing Practices to Keep Your Company Out of Court* (all AMACOM). Dr. Weiss earned his Ph.D. from Tulane University.